T0370520

The Ambassador of Loneliness

by E. Bassey

Rev. date: 08/26/2024

To order additional copies of this book, contact:
Xlibris
844-714-8691
www.Xlibris.com
Orders@Xlibris.com
862378

Acknowledgements

I am nothing...God is Everything.

"With gratitude the universe is eternally abundant."— Unknown

Introduction

Sometimes in the presence of others I can feel alone.
For most of my existence I have been an introvert.
I used to conceal this aspect of my life. However,
I've learned to embrace & love this part of my being.
I penned this book in order to creatively express
myself & share my art with others. If any readers
can identify with any of the words on these pages,
all the better. Peace, Respect and Understanding!

Contents

"A Father's Day"

As I spend the day with my child
Worries run through my crown
A series of upsets & letdowns
Far from royalty
I live by a code of loyalty
Which could result in my demise
One day I'll realize
That my heart carries too much for its size
Hopefully it won't be the reason why I die
True love can be hard to find
A good woman to hear my cries
Would I even trust her not to lie?
Do I really try?
I long for the warmth of a lady's company
Some days I've felt like a dummy
Women have spent their time for my money
Some of them have shunned me
It has ceased to stun me
Nice guys do finish last
I've never been the head of the class
Just trying to maintain my grasp

On a touch of class
Rattled nerves had me touching a glass
Filled with a drink that could make me crash
While in & out of a car
I've seen, but I haven't gone far
I never hid my scars
Exposed like the front of playing cards
I've learned to embrace my loneliness
Not varying degrees of phoniness
I believe some people love me
Although, The One that truly does is above me
So many things in my life could've went wrong
Due to Divine intervention I still stand strong
My faith in God should never waver
I can't say the same for my Earthly neighbors
Sometimes I question
Do I deserve my blessings?
Is this the quiet before the storm...
Followed by a downpour of lessons
Or maybe I'm just stressing
Over things that shouldn't hold my attention
I spend my days staving off depression

My poems are my confessions
A way to ease & release some tension
May God Bless all men
And all of our descendants.

"I Should've Known..."

I should've known better
I wrote you numerous letters
In the form of poems
Although, sent to no one
I saved myself embarrassment
You were a woman with no comparisons
Now I know what a higher standard is
I envisioned seeing you again
Why did our dating come to an end?
I didn't want to be trapped in a zone for friends
I didn't know what to believe
Maybe I was a little naive
My intentions were for your heart to be seized
Nothing worth having comes with ease
Over you I was delirious
I doubt you took me serious
Was I a joke amongst you & your buddies?
A low priority
While other guys were placed above me?
I'm trying not to develop disdain
My attempts seem to have been in vain

When you're truly interested, phone calls are made
Messages are returned, without ridiculous delays
And time together gets arranged
I'm about my business, not playing games
You don't owe me a thing
I'm not crazed
With time passed, would anything have changed
I spent more than money, but nothing was obtained
I guess we're on two different plains
Not you, only my heart is to blame
My name has become synonymous with "lame"
This is the last time I'll write about you
So that my dreams at night will be without you.

"Adored"

I'm starting to believe that love doesn't exist
Is it something of a myth?
Blessed, yet I deny myself this gift
I've always been a one woman man
However, I've been a one man band
Isolation takes a firm stand
No one takes my hand
Depression is willing to console me
But, I can't let it hold me
It will only take a toll on me
Emotionally handcuffed
Giving the filling, while I only get the crust
Same result, whether I take my time or rush
Trust appears to be flushed
Don't tell me you love me, if you don't mean it
You tell me you love me, but I can't see it
You're not in love with me, so I can't keep it
I've been honest, while you've kept secrets
In the end, I'm the only one that's cheated
When I perceive that I received it
I really don't believe it

Days & nights are depleted
Affection is needed
Something that is deeply seeded
Although, hard to uproot
When I speak, they don't accept my truth
It's exhausting demonstrating proof
I'm dependable, while others are aloof
Everything I do seems moot
I write books & no one gives a hoot
My heart makes my mind feel dumb
You can have the cake, I'm used to the crumbs.

"Cold & Distant"

I don't write this for a pity party to come rescue me
Or for loved ones to try & lecture me
In this realm my happiness is brief
My soul seeks Heaven for constant relief
Tears fall down my face like rain
My sadness is the valve that releases the pain
I'm often plagued by guilt & shame
I pray I can change
We live on a planet filled with billions
Yet, some of us feel like abandoned children
My life is a revolving door
People come in, but they don't stay long
The way we met some people would frown upon
You are a woman I couldn't put a crown upon
A queen from Hades
Your beauty made me gaze
Our encounter left me amazed
A young woman wise beyond her age
I should have left you where we played
You're one of the few reasons I wanted to stay
"Woman of God" is the meaning of your name

That's a Goddamn shame
My experiences with you left me sour
I was quick to defend your honor
I allowed you to feel empowered
You will pay a Karmic debt without dollars
Loved ones may betray you & leave you devoured
I hope you get what I've been wishing
I know good people can have bad conditions
I believe God will take the time to listen
Warmth & closeness has been missing
For that reason I remain cold & distant.

"Good End of Bad Luck"

I haven't said a prayer in a while
That's not fair to my child
To be successful, she'll need more than her smile
Patiently trying to answer her many questions
I realize I'm loading a firearm &
her mind is the weapon
When my sector appears rotten, I have to refresh it
I'll take a scoop from my pile of blessings
And sprinkle her with lessons & messages
Until her good fortune is manifested
The words that I'm jotting is an investment
I may not reap the benefits of my labor
But if she does, then a minor becomes major
I avoid placing wagers
Uncertainty is equivalent to the future's behavior
I try earnestly not to taint her
Flawed like a money laundering banker
Minus the assets
Putting her best foot forward, she
won't follow in my steps
Countless sessions I've missed

Walking outside of the order that a class sets
My wit prevents me from being hapless
With a burning desire, I remain matchless
Discarding broken dreams into an ash pit
For visionaries to seize without a catcher's mitt
Esoterically & poetically revered like Sanskrit
Life goes on, especially when you stand stiff
Truthfully, progress demands it
It's a challenge to keep hopes high, when plans dip
The downside leaves people uptight & ready to quit
Nature is both gentle & rough
So I shift like gears in a truck
Attempting to lodge at the good end of bad luck.

"Aug-Sept"

Some things are hard to believe when true
Karma will find a way to deal with you
Our "thing" wasn't governed by honesty & truth
You put on a show & disproved
Eventually, your colors bled through
I wasn't cautious of betrayal & scandal
I was broken, but still maintained a handle
My better judgment is still mad at me
My foolishness saddens me
God forbid I sink any lower
Your evil constricted me like a boa
I tried to uplift & help you grow up
I thought you were happy when I showed up
Even when I saw you with another
I was upset, but kept it undercover
Disguising yourself as my lover
However, the truth has been discovered
Moments with you made me feel lucky
I desired for you to completely trust me
People like you make this world very ugly
Hidden in a shell that appears to be lovely

Good things come to those who wait in life
I've never been the patient type
For you I made the attempt
I'm so used to settling for less
Now I'm filled with regret
Pain in the center of my chest
I rue the day we met
You claimed I was different from the rest
Because of you I rethink my steps
Venturing on my quest for happiness
I didn't expect to fall for anyone
Then along you come...tripping me up
Letting me down, instead of picking me up.

"City For Keeps"

She was there when I was born
She'll be there when I'm mourned
May our stitched connection never be torn
By myself & others she is adorned
She held me at the moment I was birthed
She'll be in the caravan that tails my hearse
When she is poorly treated, I can feel her hurt
She possess a beauty that is rarely unearthed
I tattooed her initials on my arm
I write about her, inspired by her charm
I traversed different parts of society
So I could embrace her variety
I take delight in my talks with her
I enjoy taking long walks with her
Especially when no one is around
Our beating hearts make a lovely sound
I protected her on those late evenings
I consoled her when she was grieving
I kept her warm during the cold seasons
For thirty plus years
Her tears have washed away my fears

I like it when she cries
When I wipe her eyes
I can see the sun shine
When I felt low, she has gotten me high
When others deserted me
She remained & worked with me
She introduced me to awesome people
She alerted me to the ones who were deceitful
A time will come when I have to leave her
She can never be too far for me to reach her
Because in my heart is where I'll always keep her.

"I, Poet"

I am complete & I am undone
I am many & I am none
I am the loner & I am the bunch
I am the patient & I am the rushed
I am the lover & the one that lusts
I am the over & the underachiever
I am the skeptic & I am the believer
I am human, therefore I sin
I have lost, so I know I can win
I had a beginning, ultimately I will have an end
I have been taught by the best of them
Regurgitating what I've learned through the pen
I'm the fox that hungers for the hen
I am the message that's difficult to send
I'm the broken heart that's laborious to mend
I am the cane for the strained, that's tough to bend
I'm the hand that's easy to lend
I am the time that's available to spend
I'm the enemy who needs a friend
I am the assorted techniques that seamlessly blend
I don't follow "them"

However, I am an existing trend
I am the how & the when
I am the now & the then
I am the bottom of the barrel &
the creme de la creme
I have experienced, therefore I've been
I compose, therefore I am
I am the head & the hole in it
I am the sky's limit & the depths of a pit
I am writing & the glow that's in it
I know who I am...
I am Poet.

"So Dreamy"

Fathom the true feelings of a man
I yearn for a woman to understand
At times I require a female to help me plan
Sometimes I need a lady to hold my hand
A man's ego can be fragile
The path to my love is quite narrow
Stand by me & replace my shadow
I don't require much
Intelligent conversation, intimacy & lust
No other woman could rival your touch
Kiss me on my forehead
Lay next to me in bed
Make sure my mind, body & soul is fed
Sometimes a woman is waiting to be led
Reassuring me to go where others won't tread
Correct me where I'm fallible
Mend my broken heart because it's salvageable
Time spent together is valuable
It's essential for a man to feel needed
Not emasculated or mistreated
Not forgotten about or deleted

Not kept in the dark amongst your secrets
Not competing foolishly for your affection
He can use a generous amount of your attention
Romantically reaching ascension
Replenishing his strength to slay the dragon in a fight
She motivates the knight to
traverse through the night
In order for him to return to his queen alright
If you're dishonored, he will go to war for you
When you manifest your dreams, he will applaud you
You would know he truly adores you
Because he has done everything he can for you.

"SSDD"

In my daughter's eyes & I see innocence
I look into the mirror & see filthiness
Her world is filled with opportunities
My world is filled with goals unachieved
And clouds of disbelief
Storms are caused by my mischief
I try to produce
Then my fortitude is reduced
I drop to my knees
To the Most High I plead
Daily I try to pray
Although, I'm running out of things to say
God patiently waits
For the day I change my fate
I just hope that it won't be too late
I play, but then I can't afford to pay
The Lord extends my line of credit
I am eternally & spiritually indebted
Living with actions I have regretted
Yet, not enough to be progressive
The idea of waking up is cherished

However, I'm emotionally beheaded
My skull rolls back to where it was bedded
I try to rise, but my frame is leaded
For my child's sake I leg it
My past screams at me "FORGET IT"
Because my presence is protected
My future is unknown
But when it comes I must accept it.

"Black Days & White Nights"

I've had breakfast, lunch & dinner with schmucks
I've taking a dip in Gin filled cups
I've lost valuables on unreliable trusts
As a result I don't grin much
Winning for me is tough
I gain small prizes
The big sized ones don't happen enough
I spend time, but the price keeps going up
My pen works my fingers to the bone
I maneuver through zones
Where no one roams
Loneliness vs being alone
For my past errors, this is how I atone
My consolidated theories resemble a drone
Traveling in the opposite direction of clones
I prefer to fly low
If I crash, it's not such a critical blow
Emotions are on autopilot when flown
Sometimes it's difficult to soar
Cheerfulness is locked outside the cockpit door
I choose not to ride excitement anymore

When my happiness is explored
It's usually a short tour
Too much turbulence caused by downpours
Subsequently, my joyfulness is detoured
For every vice dropped off, another seems to board
The unnecessary freight weighs me down
Elevation comes from a lyrical mound
How can a faceless person manage to frown?
Airborne feelings witnessing sensational views
Forsaken by members of my crew
People rarely share my point to rendezvous
My nightly solitude anoints me
with the morning's dew.

"Tiny Hole"

Little pieces break away from it
People have taken & walked away with it
A meager sample
Although, enough to no longer be ample
It's still beating, so there is more that it can handle
People have chipped & chipped away at it
Ripped & stripped for days at it
I know I haven't helped
Stress & bad habits have affected its health
Grief has always been felt
Even when acknowledging the
suffering of someone else
Sitting in my chest, it never rests or quits
It doesn't know what it's like to be desired
Hopefully, it will know before its retired
I've neglected it
I no longer let others mess with it
I try my best to protect & invest in it
To my detriment, I feel deep
Like scuba divers detecting coral reefs
I know it weeps

I supply comfort until the day it sleeps
It's strong, but weak at the same time
It's quiet, but speaks to my mind
Combined they both manufacture rhymes
I wonder how much my "safe place" can take
Can people really die from heartbreak?
Before it provides an escape route for my soul
I must try to clog this tiny hole.

"Track Changes & Train Scraps"

Life's science has me doing research
I traverse in my head until my feet hurt
Before stress creeps in, I try to breathe first
I sit quietly
Trying to believe there is no denying me
People enjoy lying to me
The government likes spying on me
Daily I attempt to face facts
It's hard to awake from naps
Just to rush to work and make scraps
There were times I was a sap
My spirit uses my mind for a map
Avoiding negativity so I can relax
People can be delusional
Convincing me that my truths are refutable
But, my beliefs are crucial
We live in times that are brutal
Love isn't a feeling that is mutual
Food for thought isn't thoroughly chewed
Reflecting on the days I had a slim fit
I gained weight worrying about a sick chick

She was vile
I was also concerned about my child
I felt like I lost my gifts
My Mojo was becoming stiff
My spirit became harder to lift
I had the bread and butter, but no fish
I was dimwitted
I gambled and lost chips
My allegiance was to food, liquor and cigarettes
I have fewer acquaintances & avoid relationships
Right before your eyes I can shape shift
Shedding pounds & anything else weighing me down
A grown man that can see himself & laugh
When the time asks
I can unleash my wrath
Or embrace the mass & give them my last
I chat with God while listening to Jazz
I'm the only pupil in my class
On a long run with a hallway pass.

"Mi Reina de la Crueldad"

You can't find love in unsavory places
Needs & wants hide behind tight lipped faces
Fools rush in, but it's hard to pace it
When your emotions want to taste it
Perfection is a rare thing to find
Regretting all of our shared moments combined
Physically she was well designed
Both born under the same sign
The farthest apart in personality & mind
I thought she was as precious as time
Sexy without trying
People supported her lying
I was never in her heart, but kept her in mine
Untrue to me with no hesitation
Vengeance would be a dream's manifestation
My spirit relies on Karma for relaxation
She was miles away
Managing to keep me in denial for days
She laid her head in my lap
At the drop of a hat
I sacrificed so much to share her space on maps

She was setting up traps
While using the phone to chat
She knew that she had me
I was her's as long as she'd have me
I respected her, but she had other plans for me
I never met an evil so uncanny
Deceived by she, her friends & family
That part of my existence feels so unrealistic
Now I have insight like a Mystic
My third eye had a cataract, but I fixed it
I was like a knight trying to save her
All the while, Mi Reina was putting me in danger.

"The Horror"

New York City is where this horror takes place
As a youngster, I was involved in "Child's Play"
Then I grew into a "Candyman"
I grabbed lives and held death in my hands
I took delight in this type of behavior
I was an authentic "HellRaiser"
I seasoned my prowess as a stalker
I preyed effortlessly on many a "SleepWalker"
After my victims were detained
They became "Chained" & maimed
Departing from my domain
I would catch the "Midnight Meat Train"
On a every "Friday the 13th"
I would traverse my "Dark City" from underneath
Until I reached that "Nightmare on Elm Street"
On one particular "Halloween"
I inserted my "Skeleton Key"
Into the mind of a target that trusted me
Resulting in a "PumpkinHead" seed
That grew in a "Pet Sematary"
I would invite folks to my "FunHouse"

Where a fatal "Trick or Treat"
would enter their mouths
A "Deadly Friend" that devised their end
No longer needing to pretend
"I Spit on Your Grave" & then escape
Into a Dodge Turbo Interceptor
driven by "The Wraith"
On "Prom Night" I've escorted numerous dates
Unaware a "Maniac" would lay them to waste
Bodies dumped on a "Silent Hill" in the countryside
Little did I know, "The Hills Have Eyes"
Twice a month "Sweeney Todd" cuts my hair
Then I grab drinks with "The People Under the Stairs"
I'm "DeathProof" & my condition is rare
Causing "Planet Terror" is my plan
Avoid making a "Wrong Turn" into
my "Village of the Damned"
If you can't appreciate the Horror,
then you wouldn't understand.

"Dead to the World"

Dead to the world, but no funeral
No candles, no flowers & no mural
Only a cremation of the world I once knew
A new one arises from the ashes I blew
A place where your ego isn't bruised
& it's ok to feel blue
More cloudy & less sunny
No idolizing dummies & no one goes hungry
People are more important than money
Girls don't behave manly
They're goal oriented, but also have time for family
Men don't act feminine
Doctors are genuine
And cures define modern medicine
Death must come, in order for Life to begin
It's Life that we choose to chase
While Death patiently waits
It knows it can't be escaped
Recklessness is the bait
To live or die is the great debate
I fell from Grace

Only to land on my face
Clean my slate & recalculate my fate
So I can minimize mistakes
I embrace the dark shapes
That hibernate & permeate
Where light is afraid to penetrate
Black & white thoughts I segregate
Although, they swirl
Whenever my pen twirls
And ink is hurled
Into the pages it burrows
Unselfish, so I remain for my little girl
Alive to her, but dead to the world.

"Wipeout"

Rest In Peace My Dude
You were a breath of fresh air that was cool
I can clearly recollect those days in June
We were two Virgos highly in tune
You didn't know that I would be back so soon
I can recall drinking booze under the Moon
I reminisce walking around town & having fun
I remember conversing under the Sun
You shared tales of where you came from
You listened intently & encouraged
my work that was undone
You are a hero that was unsung
I didn't know about the demons you had to overcome
You accomplished so much at an age so young
Your parents raised an A1 son
I couldn't wait to see your face again
Embrace you & shake hands like men
You imparted wisdom on me that will never leave
Your passing was something I couldn't believe
My mood changed & I began to grieve
I needed confirmation for what my eyes couldn't see

My ears were in denial
You survived so much, how could you depart now?
You were a good friend
From the start to the end
May God forever bless your children
I pray we'll all see you in Heaven
I wish that I could've helped you
Too late to shuffle the cards that life dealt you
I poured liquor in your memory
That way you could enjoy another drink with me
I hope you know you were one of the dearest
Delivered from evil, now God has your spirit.

Printed in the United States
by Baker & Taylor Publisher Services